THIS DANCE JOURNAL

BELONGS TO:

COPYRIGHT © 2022 BY KIMBERLY BECKER

ALL RIGHTS RESERVED.

HELLO, FRIENDS!

DANCING IS A WONDERFUL WAY TO EXPRESS YOURSELF WITH A PHYSICAL EXPRESSION THAT VERBAL WORDS CAN'T COMPARE TO.

DANCE AND MUSIC COMBINED TOGETHER ARE THE MOST GLORIOUS COMBINATION THAT CREATES A WAVE OF EXPRESSION THAT SIMPLY CAN'T BE MEASURED.

WHEN YOU DANCE YOU FEEL FREE.

WHEN YOU DANCE YOU FEEL EXHILIRATED.

WHEN YOU DANCE, YOU'RE SMILING FROM THE INSIDE.

WHEN THOSE FEELINGS COME TO YOU, WRITE THEM IN YOUR DANCE JOURNAL TO REMEMBER THEM FOR ALWAYS AND ALWAYS!

XOXO,
KIMBERLY ♥

I LOVE TO DANCE

DANCING IS... 'MY' EVERYTHING!

I WOULD RATHER BE DANCING!

NO TALKING — JUST DANCE!!!

DANCING IS... MY JAM!!!

IT'S DANCE OR NOTHING!

DANCE LIGHTS MUSIC ACTION

DANCING ZONE!
ONLY: MUSIC, DANCING & FUN ALLOWED!!!

DANCING IS MY FAVORITE EXPRESSION!

★ ★ ★ ★ ★ ★ ★ ★ ★ ★

I CAN FEEL THE MUSIC

MY HEART BELONGS TO DANCE

I LOVE TO DANCE

♥ ♥ ♥ ♥ ♥ ♥ ♥

♪ ♫

DANCING IS... 'MY' EVERYTHING!

I WOULD RATHER BE DANCING!

NO TALKING — JUST DANCE!!!

DANCING IS... MY JAM!!!

IT'S DANCE OR NOTHING!

DANCE LIGHTS MUSIC ACTION

DANCING ZONE!
ONLY: MUSIC, DANCING & FUN ALLOWED!!!

DANCING IS MY FAVORITE EXPRESSION!

I CAN FEEL THE MUSIC

MY HEART BELONGS TO DANCE

I LOVE TO DANCE

DANCING IS... 'MY' EVERYTHING!

★ ★ ★ ★ ★ ★ ★ ★ ★

I WOULD RATHER BE DANCING!

NO TALKING — JUST DANCE!!!

DANCING IS... MY JAM!!!

IT'S DANCE OR NOTHING!

DANCE LIGHTS MUSIC ACTION

DANCING ZONE!
ONLY: MUSIC, DANCING & FUN ALLOWED!!!

DANCING IS MY FAVORITE EXPRESSION!

★ ★ ★ ★ ★ ★ ★ ★ ★ ★ ★ ★

I CAN FEEL THE MUSIC

MY HEART BELONGS TO DANCE

I LOVE TO DANCE

DANCING IS... 'MY' EVERYTHING!

I WOULD RATHER BE DANCING!

NO TALKING JUST DANCE!!!

★ ★ ★ ★ ★ ★ ★ ★ ★ ★

DANCING IS... MY JAM!!!

IT'S DANCE OR NOTHING!

DANCE LIGHTS MUSIC ACTION

DANCING ZONE!
ONLY: MUSIC, DANCING & FUN ALLOWED!!!

DANCING IS MY FAVORITE EXPRESSION!

I CAN FEEL THE MUSIC

MY HEART BELONGS TO DANCE

I LOVE TO DANCE

DANCING IS... 'MY' EVERYTHING!

★ ★ ★ ★ ★ ★ ★ ★

I WOULD RATHER BE DANCING!

NO TALKING — JUST DANCE!!!

★ ★ ★ ★ ★ ★ ★ ★ ★ ★ ★

DANCING IS... MY JAM!!!

IT'S DANCE OR NOTHING!

DANCE LIGHTS MUSIC ACTION

DANCING ZONE!
ONLY: MUSIC, DANCING & FUN ALLOWED!!!

DANCING IS MY FAVORITE EXPRESSION!

I CAN FEEL THE MUSIC

MY HEART BELONGS TO DANCE

I LOVE TO DANCE

DANCING IS... 'MY' EVERYTHING!

I WOULD RATHER BE DANCING!

NO TALKING   **JUST DANCE!!!**

DANCING IS... MY JAM!!!

IT'S DANCE OR NOTHING!

DANCE   LIGHTS   MUSIC   ACTION

DANCING ZONE!
ONLY: MUSIC, DANCING & FUN ALLOWED!!!

DANCING IS MY FAVORITE EXPRESSION!

★ ★ ★ ★ ★ ★ ★ ★ ★ ★ ★

I CAN FEEL THE MUSIC

MY HEART BELONGS TO DANCE

I LOVE TO DANCE

DANCING IS... 'MY' EVERYTHING!

I WOULD RATHER BE DANCING!

NO TALKING JUST DANCE!!!

★ ★ ★ ★ ★ ★ ★ ★ ★ ★

DANCING IS... MY JAM!!!

IT'S DANCE OR NOTHING!

DANCE LIGHTS MUSIC ACTION

DANCING ZONE!
ONLY: MUSIC, DANCING & FUN ALLOWED!!!

DANCING IS MY FAVORITE EXPRESSION!

★ ★ ★ ★ ★ ★ ★ ★ ★ ★ ★

I CAN FEEL THE MUSIC

MY HEART BELONGS TO DANCE

I LOVE TO DANCE

DANCING IS... 'MY' EVERYTHING!

I WOULD RATHER BE DANCING!

NO TALKING JUST DANCE!!!

DANCING IS... MY JAM!!!

IT'S DANCE OR NOTHING!

DANCE LIGHTS MUSIC ACTION

DANCING ZONE!
ONLY: MUSIC, DANCING & FUN ALLOWED!!!

DANCING IS MY FAVORITE EXPRESSION!

I CAN FEEL THE MUSIC

MY HEART BELONGS TO DANCE

I LOVE TO DANCE

DANCING IS... 'MY' EVERYTHING!

I WOULD RATHER BE DANCING!

NO TALKING JUST DANCE!!!

★ ★ ★ ★ ★ ★ ★ ★ ★ ★ ★

DANCING IS... MY JAM!!!

IT'S DANCE OR NOTHING!

DANCE MUSIC LIGHTS ACTION

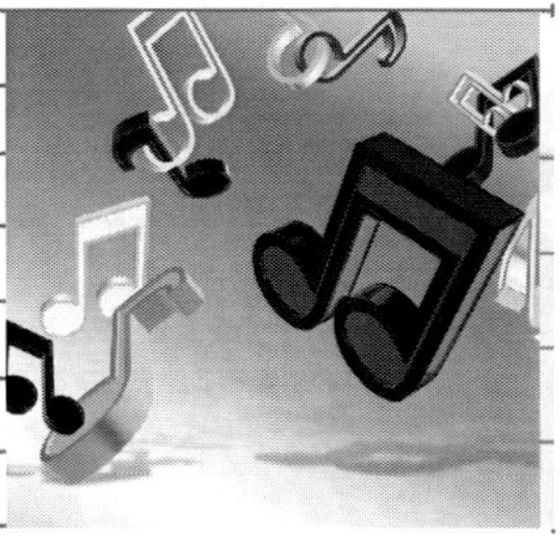

DANCING ZONE!
ONLY: MUSIC, DANCING & FUN ALLOWED!!!

MY HEART BELONGS TO DANCE

I
LOVE

LOVE

LOVE

TO

DANCE!

DANCING IS... 'MY' EVERYTHING!

I WOULD RATHER BE DANCING!

NO TALKING JUST DANCE!!!

DANCING IS... MY JAM!!!

IT'S DANCE OR NOTHING!

DANCE LIGHTS MUSIC ACTION

DANCING ZONE!
ONLY: MUSIC, DANCING & FUN ALLOWED!!!

DANCING IS MY FAVORITE EXPRESSION!

I CAN FEEL THE MUSIC

MY HEART BELONGS TO DANCE

I LOVE TO DANCE

DANCING IS... 'MY' EVERYTHING!

I WOULD RATHER BE DANCING!

NO TALKING   JUST DANCE!!!

DANCING IS... MY JAM!!!

IT'S DANCE OR NOTHING!

DANCE LIGHTS MUSIC ACTION

DANCING ZONE!
ONLY: MUSIC, DANCING & FUN ALLOWED!!!

MY HEART BELONGS TO DANCE

I
LOVE

LOVE

LOVE

TO

DANCE!

Manufactured by Amazon.ca
Acheson, AB